Cheaper Easier Direct
How to Disrupt the Marketplace and
Create Your Own E-Commerce Empire

Authors:
Chad Rubin and Frank Turner

All contents Copyright © 2016 by Chad Rubin

ISBN: 978-0-692-71332-7

HOW TO DISRUPT THE MARKETPLACE AND
CREATE YOUR OWN E-COMMERCE EMPIRE

CHEAPER

EASIER

DIRECT

CHAD

RUBIN

CEO OF CRUCIAL VACUUM AND SKUBANA
WITH FRANK TURNER

"THE UNIVERSE IS EXCEEDINGLY GENEROUS. WHEN A FARMER SOWS ONE SEED, A PLANT COMES FORTH THAT PRODUCES THOUSANDS OF SEEDS. IF YOU DESIRE ABUNDANCE, BE LIKE THE FARMER AND FIRST GIVE UP SOMETHING. WHATEVER YOU RECEIVE, KEEP A PORTION FOR YOURSELF AND SHARE A PORTION WITH OTHERS. BY ESTABLISHING YOURSELF IN THE FLOW OF GENEROSITY, WHATEVER YOU GIVE WILL COME BACK MANIFOLD."

SWAMI KRIPALU (1913 – 1981),
WHOSE LIFE AND TEACHINGS
INSPIRE ME IN BUSINESS AND LIFE.

It means a hell of a lot to me that you acquired this book in either print or digital format.

As a thank you for buying this book, please pick up my free toolkit, Amazon Mastery: 10 Crucial Strategies from a Top 200 Seller. ecommercerenegade.com/bonus, to help you avoid mistakes when using the world's top online store.

TABLE OF CONTENTS

INTRODUCTION:

THE LAST
THING I EVER
WANTED

"THERE'S A DIFFERENCE BETWEEN KNOWING THE PATH AND WALKING THE PATH."

MORPHEUS,
THE MATRIX

Entrepreneurs? Those are the most broke, starving, struggling bunch of bums on the face of the Earth. Don't ever go into business for yourself. You'll always be in debt. You'll always be a loser.

That's what I would have told you up until just a handful of years ago. Unlike many Americans, I didn't yearn to be the next Jobs, Gates, Branson, Trump, or Zuckerberg. I craved stability. From as early as I can remember my parents struggled to make their vacuum store stay afloat – and like too many Americans, we lived from one credit card statement to the next. I remember going to the grocery store with my mom who would whip out a dozen credit cards at checkout, handing them over one-by-one until the cashiers found one that wasn't maxed out. The people in line behind us just had to wait. The terms "entrepreneur," "self-employed," and "business owner" gave me the chilliest of chills; I didn't want to live like this.

Decades later, I would be laid off from my job and end up selling, of all things, vacuum parts on the internet. It turns out I was one of the first people to do so. Before I knew it, I assumed the very job title I had run from, an "entrepreneur," specifically an "e-commerce entrepreneur."

So what the hell happened?

It was 2008 and I had been working for a Wall Street firm researching e-commerce and making stock recommendations. The hours were *punishing,* usually from 7 am until 2 am, and despite my hustle, my boss and I would often butt heads about where clients should put their money. This constant disagreement led to my getting sacked, and suddenly I had the daunting task of looking for work at a time when no one on The Street was hiring. Yet, despite the need to pay my bills, the idea of going on a job-search felt like torture. Instead, I felt the pull to help my parents who were still struggling with their vacuum store. It occurred to me that I could start putting some of my internet research skills towards helping them sell their goods online.

So why weren't my parents already selling their vacuum accessories on the internet? Well, because it was foreign to them. So my first effort at e-commerce was born. I created a site called KillDirt to sell their inventory online and it was an instant success.

I could not believe it. Yet the deeper I got with this venture, the more opportunity I saw. For instance, I noticed that my parents were wasting money getting their supplies from distributors rather than directly from manufacturers. I wanted to start getting parts made for me, under my own name brand, and start selling directly to consumers. Today, it's cool to be a direct-to-consumer company like Warby Parker, Everlane, Dollar Shave Club, and dozens more. But in 2009, **nobody** was doing it, so it was scary, or a word I love more: *disruptive.* My parents were thrilled with how KillDirt was going, so I handed the reins over to them entirely. It was time for me to start my own venture, *Crucial Vacuum.*

I stood staring up at a massive challenge and opportunity: How could I get the same vacuum accessories that manufacturers made, skip the middleman distributor, and sell directly to the consumer on the internet at a lower price? Believe it or not, back then, the major brands refused to sell directly to me. They were scared. This is a good lesson: when people are scared and refuse to do business with you, it means you're on to something. So I went to Asia, had my own products built, and after a lot of hard work and mistakes, I managed to disrupt the vacuum space. Since that initial venture, I have moved on to other industries ripe for disruption by creating Crucial Coffee, Crucial Air, Think Crucial, and now, Skubana, a platform for anyone to run their own e-commerce company end-to-end. In 2015, my company's value was over $20 million (with only 6 employees[1]) and there is much more

---

[1] Take note: Most people judge a company's success by how many employees they have but it's quite the opposite. More employees = more expenses and people to manage. Every time I go to a party and people find out I am an entrepreneur, that's their first question: how many employees do I have? It's the wrong question.

in our sights to disrupt.

I've come to deeply embrace my entrepreneurial identity – the hustle and hard work can, in fact, be rewarded with riches, but also with freedom and the power to create your own future. I realize now that I was destined for this life, and that getting laid off when I did was the biggest blessing the universe could have ever given me. At the same time, I've seen many people lose their shirts or barely tread water in e-commerce, and like my parents, those who keep failing are often the hardest working and the most earnest in their efforts.

Unfortunately, it's often the really minute decisions that can cost you a fortune in business, but this is never truer than in e-commerce. Despite that warning, I assure you that if you want to be in business for yourself, there is truly no better place than e-commerce. The start-up capital you need is small compared to most industries and not only can you make a killing, but you will see that the world needs your disruption. The masses are *begging* for it. No one wants to pay $12 for a three-pack of razor blades after waiting for a minimum wage employee at a chain drugstore to unlock them when they can get the same quality razors for $3 sent directly to their home. The world has never been more ready to say goodbye to these dumb business models – and know that there are dumb, useless business models everywhere. They are dying to be flipped on their heads and swept aside by something smarter, simpler, and more affordable.

I wrote this book because I've run into many rough patches over my last eight years as an entrepreneur, and I want to help you avoid them. With this book, you will be able to use and reference my formula for disruptive e-commerce success. However, this is a guide book not a paint-by-numbers manual like many e-commerce courses provide. They'll have you selling spatulas on Amazon for a few cents cheaper than your neighbor. No, every step in my process is a part of a formula that's been tested numerous times, and yet is still broad enough for you to apply to your own tastes and interests. It doesn't matter if you hate coffee and home goods: you will be able to apply these steps and tools to any e-commerce venture.

In fact, that would thrill me more than anything – run with this book and disrupt industries that people said couldn't be changed. This book is your guide. It will take you from e-commerce inspiration, all the way to having your own successful product in the hands of a satisfied customer.

This book that you have before you will revolutionize how you do business, making you a more successful and productive seller. I applaud you for taking this journey and I am honored to be a part of it.

Looking forward,
Chad Rubin

PART 1: DISCOVERY

COMBINING WHAT YOU'RE PASSIONATE ABOUT WITH WHAT PISSES YOU OFF

CHAPTER 1

WHAT BOTHERS YOU?

Take a look at your life right now and think about what frustrates you. What annoys you every time you think about it because you know it could be different and better? Don't take the bird's eye view, that will simply generate broad and bland gripes: *I want more money, I want sex/love/a relationship, I want to be happy.* These eternal yearnings will not be solved by any Silicon Valley geniuses or Harvard MBAs. Instead, what you want is a magnifying glass over your life, or a look at your day as if you were watching it on a security camera – one that zooms in and out as needed.

What irritates you? In the answer to this question lies a vein of *gold.* Take something in your life that bugs you, the exorbitant cost of compression socks for runners, for example. *Why do they cost $50 a pair?* Well, there's a pretty good chance that many other people have that same feeling, and would buy your answer to the problem. It's in the mundane and the tedious that you can create simple solutions which will allow millions of people to save time and money, and pat themselves on the back for doing so. They might even tell their friends to be just as cool and smart as they are. Can you imagine physically travelling to a video rental store now to simply return a DVD? Can you imagine doing so in the middle of a snowstorm, rushing to get it back before midnight to avoid paying a late fee? Yeah, I can't either. Since the dawn of Netflix, that idea feels like it's from the 1800s.

Or let's say you're with your friend who's moaning about having lost her glasses and having to drop a couple hundred bucks to go to a rip-off optometrist for sizing and a new pair. *What? Why? Has she not heard of Warby Parker?* She can look online for prescription glasses that are shipped to her home five at a time and with no upfront charges. And when she's ready to buy a pair, they cost a fraction of what they would at any retail optometrist. These ideas were all the mundane pet peeves of entrepreneurs who actually set out to solve the problem. What's your gripe?

You don't want to reinvent the wheel and spend years and reams of your and other people's money on the next great new technology or business. Rather, how can you simplify the lives of others and save them some cash in the process? When I first launched my own direct-to-consumer vacuum store online, I thought that was all I would ever do; I would be an online vacuum accessories merchant for the rest of my life. The impact of Crucial Vacuum was so swift and massive, and grabbed such a huge chunk of that market, that I started thinking about what else I could do.

One of my biggest passions was coffee, and I noticed that not only were coffee filters expensive, but often not reusable. So Crucial Coffee was born. The first product we manufactured was a reusable stainless steel filter to be used with the Aerobie AeroPress coffee maker. If you love coffee like I do, why should you constantly be ordering one-time use filters which is a waste of time, money, and paper? How about using a stainless steel filter instead that is inexpensive, high quality, and saves coffee lovers time and money? It's what people needed, so I created it.

Take a look at your life.
Jot down 5 things that piss you off.
There's a decent chance they piss others off as well.

Ideally, this brainstorm should focus on things you are familiar with or are passionate about. Right off the top of my head, I can think of a few annoyances for which I would love to see an e-commerce solution. One of my passions is CrossFit, but I hate that CrossFit shorts tend to cost anywhere from $50 to $250! Similarly, my wife teaches yoga, so I've become familiar with that world: someone tell me why Lululemon yoga pants cost $120. They're great, but like all exercise clothes, they take a beating, and then you need new ones. These are two great examples of huge opportunities for someone to provide the same or better quality at a much cheaper price.

Of course, it doesn't have to be an item you buy in a store. This is the *discovery* process and it's what led to the creation of Skubana, my end-to-end e-commerce software company I built with my partner, DJ Kunovac. At the end of this book is an addendum that explains how Skubana works and how it can benefit your e-commerce business. It was immensely frustrating trying to run Crucial Vacuum on various fragmented tools when none of them communicated with each other. I wanted one solution to run everything and automate my business. This one time, pre-Skubana, we got a ton of Crucial Vacuum orders on Amazon and we thought we had sufficient inventory to ship. But our supply was actually below what had been purchased. Amazon penalized me for overselling and my seller account was temporarily shut down. *That sucked.* I knew I had a real problem that others were experiencing and **no one could properly solve.** And so Skubana was born to solve the headaches we had at Crucial Vacuum in working with multiple applications that didn't work with one another.

☑

CHAPTER 2

DOES MY PRODUCT SOLVE A PROBLEM?

A lot of people talk to me about their passions and ideas, but sometimes they don't translate into something that others want. You may have a clever idea for a type of mug or a uniquely flavored mint, or perhaps something that creates nostalgia for your childhood, but how many people also want it?

A great way to validate an idea, of course, is to do research. Beyond talking to friends about your idea, you should hit the internet like it's your job, and in a sense, it is. Does anything like your product exist on Amazon, Newegg, Rakuten, or elsewhere? Sometimes, you just want to see how much demand there is. We knew that AeroPress coffee makers were in high demand simply by their best-selling rank on Amazon and we found repeated reviews from customers who desired better filters. Reading the reviews on Amazon, particularly the negative reviews, helps you identify the problems with a great product. What is the product narrative from your customers or, better yet, your competitors' customers?

AeroPress' filter stood out as a key complaint to an otherwise universally beloved product. The question then became: how could we develop a reusable one? Before we began researching, another key concern was what I call the **"Amazon Product Death Cycle"** of the AeroPress. It's the time until the product gets to maturation, and it's not nearly as popular as it once was and then dies off. Before you even hit that point, you should always go where the puck goes. *Huh?* It's a quote by Hall of Fame hockey player Wayne Gretzky: "I skate to where the puck is going to be, not where it has been." The AeroPress wasn't new when we began looking into making reusable filters, but their fan base was rabid and had been consistently active since the product's debut several years earlier. Every year since 2008, fans of the AeroPress have gone so far as to hold the World AeroPress Championships (worldaeropresschampionship.com). These worldwide competitions to make the best tasting cup of coffee using an AeroPress are treated with the seriousness of a professional boxing match and held in countries like Australia, Japan, Italy and many others. *Can you name another coffee maker whose fans do that?* The AeroPress is given such respect that, despite its design for home use, there is an extensive list of cafes around the world that use the AeroPress as an in-house coffee maker. It became a must for us to design a reusable filter for this treasured tool among java heads.

One has to try and distinguish between the low and steady flame of popularity from a *niche fan base* and the so-hot-you'll-get-burned sparks of what's popular *right now.* That usually means you have to invest in products that everyone is not investing in. If you are doing what others are doing, how will you ever win? That's why reading reviews is so important: go after sub-niches, niches of niches, go where the puck is going.

As of the writing of this book (Spring 2016), electric skateboards and hoverboards get hits o'plenty on online shopping sites. But despite their being featured in almost every holiday gift guide, their retail price has been on a **steady decline.** About a year ago, the retail price for a hoverboard was floating around $700, but now you can easily get the same board for $200. So, rather than make another hoverboard, how about a travel bag for it? A travel bag solves a precise need for hoverboard owners without competing with everyone else selling the commoditized full-unit.

Similarly, how scalable is your idea, and can it be developed into a brand? If you were to make travel bags for electric skateboards, could you also branch into bags for snowboards and surfboards? Or perhaps develop home storage units that display skateboards and the like, allowing a skater to quickly grab a board off the wall and go riding? You want something that can grow.

It became a natural move for my team to move into coffee accessories, Crucial Coffee, and later air filters, Crucial Air, and now we are looking at anything that is considered crucial to the home with Think Crucial. As you can see, this is a fully developed concept and brand. Customers now come back to us to see what we have that's new; they want to buy from us before going elsewhere.

"THERE'S NO VALUE IN DIGGING SHALLOW WELLS IN A HUNDRED PLACES. DECIDE ON ONE PLACE AND DIG DEEP. EVEN IF YOU ENCOUNTER A ROCK, USE DYNAMITE AND KEEP GOING DOWN. IF YOU LEAVE THAT TO DIG ANOTHER WELL, ALL THE FIRST EFFORT IS WASTED AND THERE IS NO PROOF YOU WON'T HIT ROCK AGAIN."

SWAMI SATCHIDANANDA
IN HIS UPDATE OF THE YOGA SUTRAS OF PATANJALI

CHAPTER 3

THE HOLY MANTRA — BETTER, CHEAPER, EASIER & DIRECT

Look at some of the ideas for products you've jotted down and ask, *do they solve a problem?* Or in geeky business lingo: What is your product's value proposition? And how is it different from what is currently available?

Answering this question requires my mantra and a key theme of this book: Does your product make someone's life *Better, Cheaper, Easier and Direct?* Here's a quick elaboration on the meaning of these words: Your product *must* improve upon and be *better* than whatever a consumer is already using. There are many products and services that we rely on and love that could be that much better. If it isn't immediately obvious how your product or service is superior to what is already on the market, it will be a tough sell to consumers. That improvement might simply come in providing something that is loved at a lower or *cheaper* price. Note that in using *cheaper* we don't want to cheapen anyone's quality of life, but simply save them money, make their life more cost-efficient. In other instances, you might be saving someone time and creating convenience and thus making their life a little *easier.* And in terms of making a person's life *direct* – how can you get what a person wants *directly* to them, saving them money, time, and effort?

You should remember the *Better, Cheaper, Easier and Direct* mantra when looking at your or other products out there. How many of these words describe the potential product? If someone can take or leave your product when it's presented against other alternatives, it's probably not making their life much better, cheaper, easier or direct.

The most important word is *Direct.* Getting your product straight from the factory to the consumers is important because usually you are getting it to them at far cheaper than what they would pay for retail. You're also getting it to them much easier by having it delivered straight to their home.

From a seller's perspective, going directly to the consumer is far superior to selling through retail because you can get your business and sales going immediately. You aren't waiting for a retail chain's buyers to approve the introduction of your merchandise and aren't limited by the quantity they want to sell nor are you subject to how your product is placed on display in the store or how it's advertised. Most importantly, the profit margin is far greater when you are selling direct to the consumer because a third party isn't taking a cut. You're getting the product at a low price and getting it to customers far cheaper than they would pay elsewhere, most likely in a retail shop: everyone is happy.

CASE STUDIES

"IT AIN'T TO PLAY GAMES WITH YOU, IT'S TO AIM AT YOU, PROBABLY MAIM YOU."

JAY-Z,
"ENCORE"

This book is about disruption. It's about taking business models that, no matter how big or rich they have made their owners, are dumb today, and deserve to be flipped like a pancake. The direct-to-consumer revolution is doing just that. See in the subsequent case studies how total unknowns have disrupted massive industries by delivering products that are *Better, Cheaper, Easier and Direct.*

CASE STUDY #1: BONOBOS

www.bonobos.com

Bonobos is primarily a men's clothing company that set out to solve a real problem: a lack of well-fitting pants for men in American stores. The founders first targeted former athletes, specifically lacrosse players, who typically have muscular thighs and have to buy baggy or box-like pants merely to avoid having their thighs constricted. These guys were tired of feeling like they were wearing clown pants when they got dressed to go out. I also have large thighs and relate to this frustration completely. If you think about how many men there are in the US alone with bulkier thighs due to playing sports and working out, that's a huge segment of the population that could benefit this solution.

The founders then created lines of pants with different cuts for a variety of bodies and tastes including what they call their athletic cut – and the company has had massive success expanding into almost every aspect of menswear, even creating clothes for women. Let's look at how Bonobos meets the criteria of *Better, Cheaper, Easier and Direct:*

Better: They made better fitting pants not available elsewhere.

Easier: They save you a trip to the store, have great customer support, and have free shipping and returns.

Direct: They're a direct-to-consumer company, so they go straight from the factory.

You can see what's missing here: Cheaper. While not exorbitant, Bonobos isn't cheap. Men's chinos run at $88 and men's jeans jump to $120. Few can buy their clothes with any regularity, and thus their consumer base is limited. That should signal to you *an opportunity*. Bonobos isn't completely fulfilling my e-commerce holy mantra – maybe you can.

CASE STUDY #2: WARBY PARKER

www.warbyparker.com

I mentioned Warby Parker in the first chapter. They've revolutionized the eyeglass industry – which had been long overdue for disruption. The industry had been monopolized by Italy's Luxottica, which owns Lenscrafters, Sunglass Hut, Pearle Vision, Sears Optical, Target Optical, the Eyemed vision care plan, Glasses.com, Ray-Ban, Persol, and Oakley. Whew, are you surprised to learn all of these retail stores and brands fall under one giant parent company? Unfortunately, such monopolies are common today, and the parent company usually plays it smart by keeping the respective names of the brands and chains it acquires to give us the illusion of choice. Find and watch the 60 Minutes episode on Luxottica if you want more detailed info on this near monopoly.

Before Warby Parker, buying designer glasses often cost around $400, but now they cost just under $100, and best of all, they send the glasses to your home, up to five pairs to try on at a time before you buy, and, again, without any shipping costs. This is a pretty easy case study because Warby Parker hits all the targets of *Better, Cheaper, Easier and Direct.* They also have a social mission which is their *buy a pair, give a pair.* They donate a pair of eyeglasses to someone who can't afford them for every pair that's purchased.

Warby Parker is revolutionary beyond how they lowered the cost of eyeglasses. Before Warby Parker, it was assumed that eyeglass fittings had to be done in a specific physical location in the same way one views going to a hair salon for a haircut or to a mechanic to have your oil changed. Before, if you didn't live near an eyeglass store or have the time to go to one, you were screwed. The company is also truly **tech-oriented** which saves them and their customers time: The Warby Parker website is camera-enabled so you can try on glasses virtually before ordering.

Better: Convenience + Price + Virtual Reality Tech

Cheaper: Massive slashing of price bloat of old brick and mortar eyeglass companies.

Easier: They save you a trip to the store and give free shipping and returns.

Direct: They're a direct-to-consumer company so they go straight from the factory.

Frankly, this company is crushing it. Warby Parker solves a problem, but it also has built a competitive moat protecting their business with logistics. Getting their eyewear to the consumer has made it very difficult for others to compete.

CASE STUDY #3: DOLLAR SHAVE CLUB

www.dollarshaveclub.com

Like Warby Parker, Dollar Shave Club has also revolutionized its industry – razor blades. The standard model for buying razors prior to Dollar Shave Club (DSC) was that you went to a pharmacy, and then you had to ask one of the employees to come open a locked glass case and give you a packet of razors. The razors are always locked away because they are easy to steal. And *why* might they be tempting to steal? Their exorbitant price! A palm-sized pack of shaving cartridges for men typically costs anywhere from $10 to $20 with a razor handle often running from $5 to $10.

The guys at Dollar Shave Club knew what so many knew: this model is a waste of time and a total rip off. Blade buying is not a very dynamic shopping experience: guys and gals go to the store every month to get the same exact blades they did last month. So, DSC decided to eliminate that monotonous monthly trip. It had razors made in Asia and created a subscription service that sends you new razor blade cartridges in the mail every month. They took a dumb product and made it smart! The best part is the price. Rather than $10 to $20, a pack of cartridges from Dollar Shave Club is $1, $6 or $9 a month, depending on the style of cartridge you choose. Its $6 and $9 packets come with free shipping, and all of these models include a free handle. Every company dreams of generating recurring revenue from customers, and Dollar has made its value so great that it's really hard to justify cancelling a subscription. If you subscribe to Netflix and realize you never bother to use it, you might cancel. Presumably, though, if you shave with any regularity, you will always need new blades.

Better: Convenience + Price

Cheaper: Waaay cheaper than similar razors bought in stores.

Easier: No needless trips to the store as well as a convenient subscription service.

Direct: They're a direct-to-consumer company so they go straight from the factory.

In an unbelievably short time (they were founded in 2011), DSC upended the men's razor blade industry. It now has roughly 10% of the men's shaving market, which is a $13 billion-a-year industry. It's worth noting that Dollar Shave Club had a fantastic guerilla marketing campaign with hilarious videos posted to YouTube that mocked the seriousness of razor blade ads of yesteryear. This netted them 12,000 subscribers within the first two days. Their online and offline (on podcasts) ads continue using comedy so now consumers are not only getting a deal, but they're buying into a brand with a cool identity rather than another bland corporation.

CASE STUDY #4: CRUCIAL VACUUM

www.crucialvacuum.com

Okay, let's take a look at my first company, Crucial Vacuum. You already know that we are direct – our product goes from factories in Asia straight to you. Because of that, we can provide a far cheaper product than what you find at on-or-offline retail stores. You also know that we offer free shipping and returns, making it even easier and cheaper for the consumer. But then we make our products *better* by making the majority of our filters washable and reusable so that our customers get way more bang for their buck than they would shopping from other brands.

We wanted our filters to be reusable not just to save our users money, but also to help the environment, which is important to me and to everyone on my team. In thinking about how else Crucial Vacuum could have a positive impact on the planet, we came up with a social mission to plant a tree for every thousand filters that we sell. Looking solely at the reusable filter from a business perspective, I've been asked why I would build a company around a product that customers don't buy over and over again as one does with paper filters. Part of the answer is that I can sell it at a higher price point than something that's immediately disposable. The other more important element is that we create alternatives where there are none. Imagine if there was Coke but no Pepsi – you have a Dyson vacuum cleaner and want to find a replacement part without having to pay a retailer top dollar. That's where Crucial comes in.

Better: Convenience + Price + Less Environmental Impact
Cheaper: Saves you money in both short and long run.
Easier: No trip to the store and no need to keep reordering filters.
Direct: Direct-to-consumer company so the consumer pockets the savings.

Just like Bonobos moved beyond pants to sell a whole line of menswear, or Dollar Shave Club with its shave butter, we've reached into other industries with Crucial Coffee and Crucial Air, our line of air purifiers and clean air supplies. We deliver products that are better, cheaper, and easier for the consumer. Note that when I started these companies, I didn't have the cash for an extensive line of offerings. With Crucial Coffee, we started by offering one filter, a reusable one to fit the Aeropress Coffee Maker. But that single product was enough to get the business going.

I stress that people should build broad brands. Vacuum filters make for a narrow industry, and is also not the sexiest arena to be in. In retrospect, my vision was limited when I launched Crucial Vacuum. Understand that with each name brand (Crucial Vacuum, Crucial Coffee, and Crucial Air) one has to have a separate social media presence, separate emails and so on, which is a lot of work. It's far easier to do like Bonobos and keep growing under a single name. My team is now building our final version of my company called Think Crucial, which will house all of the different brands we manage as well as offer anything that's crucial for the home.

The biggest take-away with these case studies should be that consumers are willing to embrace superior products and experiences, and completely let go of standard business models that many had assumed were unshakeable. It is also clear that large existing markets are ripe for disruption by tech-enabled companies that create new ways to serve customers. I've found that successful direct-to-consumer companies generally find a way to redirect existing purchasing behavior by providing a superior customer experience. Rather than introducing something foreign and new to the market, the smart and successful e-commerce players are bringing popular products to you in a way that is infinitely more pleasing. The good news for you as a seller is: e-commerce is still quite new, and there are myriad industries that are ripe for disruption and offer low-hanging fruit. If something as simple as $1 razor blade cartridges can turn a company overnight into a valuation of hundreds of millions, then that shows you how much the traditional business model of *factory to distributor to retail* is ready to be rocked.

Let me be a little repetitive because I can't overstate this: this is the best time to start an e-commerce business. NOW. Opportunity for disruption is everywhere. We're in the midst of a profound structural shift going from institutionalized layers of middlemen to companies going directly to the consumer. And it's happening in all industries. Up until now, it's been a terribly inefficient model of factory to brand manufacturer to distributor to retailer. For every step in the chain, there is a delay and a markup. The holy grail of any business (old school or new) is to put yourself on the pulse of what consumers want. Thankfully, as an e-commerce entrepreneur you don't have the baggage of bureaucracy and people to please and pay. You can be sleek and streamlined.

There are many companies enjoying massive direct-to-consumer success in e-commerce. Here are a few others to show you the diversity of products being offered: *Casper,* a directly to consumer mattress company, *Capsule Wallets,* which makes thin wallets, and *Hello Flo,* which began as a subscription service for tampons that arrive in sync with a subscriber's cycle. These companies have all disrupted their respective industries. And *Everlane,* a clothing company, is revolutionary; their website is totally transparent about their costs and how much they charge the consumer versus what competitors, say J. Crew or Banana Republic, charge.

All of the companies discussed in these case studies have created a new marketplace for themselves. Their offerings stand out among mass-market goods to the point that not only do they bypass brick-and-mortar retail, but they aren't even competing with Amazon. Much of this book is dedicated to having success on Amazon, but it's worth noting that if you own the design and manufacturing of your product like Warby and Bonobos, you can skip Amazon all together. And much like a local fashion designer, you can offer ever more detailed small-batch niche goods. Want to do a limited run of a product? By going direct you can, and your customers will love you for it. Or maybe you just want to do a quick test of a new offering to see what the response is before launching it on Amazon and the other major channels. In developing your own brand and going direct, you create your own cosmos and can cultivate a cool factor that doesn't exist naturally on Amazon.

Remember that each of these companies is solving a real problem, and that is the essence of disruption. Most people starting e-commerce companies are not solving a problem. Instead, they are going after industries that are commoditized and not unique. There are thousands of spatulas now being sold on Amazon. The long-game is building unique products with a competitive moat that are not easy to reproduce. Lots of e-commerce guru hucksters are selling you bullshit – they tell you to become a private label at a certain weight, at a certain price point, to go after a certain category, or go after products that have a certain BSR (Best Selling Rank) and it's created an army of everyone doing the same thing. Again, you can't win if you are doing what everyone is doing.

If you want to disrupt an industry, you have to take your rival's products and strengths and do them better. When people tell me their e-commerce ideas, they often aren't providing a solution to a problem. E-commerce courses give you the paint-by-numbers approach of finding a cheap product that falls in a certain weight category, costs between $9 and $14 dollars and is made in China but that has nothing to do with fixing a problem. It doesn't matter if you can get paper clips made cheaper, for instance, if no one is complaining about the cost of paper clips.

Note that with Crucial Vacuum and the other companies in these case studies, **no one is reinventing the wheel.** Rather, each company is doing a variation on what exists, just offering a better and cheaper version of it and getting it to you in a way that's easier for you.

Let's review:
- **Find Problems Before Generating Ideas**
- **Use the Holy Mantra: Better Cheaper Easier and Direct.**
- **Focus on What You Know: Your Passions**
- **Keep it Simple: Go For Low Hanging Fruit**

You're not trying to be the next Twitter, Facebook or Instagram.

Your idea shouldn't require tons of start-up capital or a large team of people.

Don't try to reinvent the wheel.

Up Next...
VALIDATION!

PART 2: VALIDATION

(OR...
WORKING
BACKWARDS
TO FIND
YOUR
AUDIENCE)

!

CHAPTER 4

FINDING THE PAIN POINT

If *Discovery* is the appetizer of my recipe for finding a great e-commerce business, then Validation is the main course. In e-commerce, you want to find products that will scale; that have the built-in potential for high growth. Basically, validation is a process of reverse engineering or playing detective to see what products people already like and then what aspects of those products could be improved.

There are three main platforms that I use to do product validation:
- Amazon
- eBay
- Google Adwords

A little over 40% of all consumers start their searches on Amazon. You always want to start your research there and eventually you will start your sales there, but we'll get to that later on with *Execution*. The other tools I use account for the bulk of other places consumers look for products online: Terapeak allows you to spy on seller data on eBay, and then Google Adwords allows you to track searches on Google.

I greatly encourage you to test out the following validation methods which you can do from any computer. Let's begin with the king, Amazon, and I'll show you exactly how I got to first selling Aeropress coffee filters. Go to Amazon.com and simply type the word *coffee* into the search bar. As the search recognizes the word it will offer a specific department like *Home and Kitchen*. So, as a test, choose that category. Then you want to sort the results since several hundred pages of items will be generated. In the upper right corner you can sort by relevance, price, average customer reviews or by *featured* – always go with featured, which is Amazon's lingo for *best selling* and that's actually what they used to call that category.

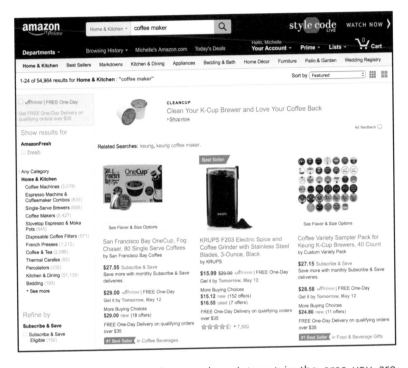

This is where it's key to have a deep interest in the area you are investigating because you want to spend a lot of time simply getting a feel for what's popular and what is new and trending. By doing searches and reading reviews on Amazon, I can figure out what is popular and what fans of those products wish could be improved. I just did a search for coffee and see assorted single cup or K-Cup brewing systems and flavored coffees meant for the Keurig coffee machines, Nespresso single-cup brewers and coffee cups, a mug warmer *(who knew?)*, espresso beans, coffee grinders, hot cocoa, a Belgian waffle maker, and so on. Note that anything at all on the first page has tremendous traction, but really, anything on the first 30 pages is quite hot. But by the same token, if you only use Amazon's Bestseller Ranking, then you will always target the same items as everyone else. If you are doing what others do, how will you win? I find items on Amazon to improve upon by getting lost on the site. I go super deep trying to find the super obscure items.

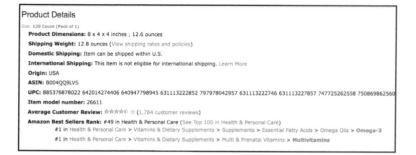

Product Details

Size: 120 Count (Pack of 1)

Product Dimensions: 8 x 4 x 4 inches ; 12.6 ounces

Shipping Weight: 12.8 ounces (View shipping rates and policies)

Domestic Shipping: Item can be shipped within U.S.

International Shipping: This item is not eligible for international shipping. Learn More

Origin: USA

ASIN: B004QQ9LVS

UPC: 885376878022 642014274406 640947798945 631113222852 797978042957 631113222746 631113227857 747725262558 750869862560

Item model number: 26611

Average Customer Review: ★★★★☆ (1,784 customer reviews)

Amazon Best Sellers Rank: #49 in Health & Personal Care (See Top 100 in Health & Personal Care)

  #1 in Health & Personal Care > Vitamins & Dietary Supplements > Supplements > Essential Fatty Acids > Omega Oils > **Omega-3**

  #1 in Health & Personal Care > Vitamins & Dietary Supplements > Multi & Prenatal Vitamins > **Multivitamins**

I've added a screenshot of a *best sellers rank* for omega fish oil. *Best sellers rank* (BSR) is a small section in the middle of a product listing page – it's a snapshot in time and changes constantly. In this case, these fish oil vitamins are ranked #47 in the entire Health and Personal category– meaning 46 products are better ranked and sell more. It's also #1 in Omega-3 category. Pretty damn good! There are millions of products worse than this that also have devoted consumers.

About half the way down on the first page of this Amazon search is the Aeropress Coffee and Espresso Maker, a bizarre almost surgical looking pump and filter coffee system with nearly 5000 reviews and almost all of them are rated excellent. After a little bit of time on Amazon, you'll see that 5000 is a ton of reviews. Most customers don't leave reviews of products, and they certainly don't rave about coffee makers, but clearly owners of the Aeropress do. If you scroll down on an item's page, under the section titled Product Details, Amazon tells you how well an item is selling. As of the writing of this eBook, the Aeropress Coffee and Espresso Maker was #28 in the entire Kitchen & Dining category and #1 in Espresso Machine & Coffeemaker Combo category! This coffeemaker that no one has ever heard of, aside from devout coffee lovers, is simply killing it.

Aeropress Coffee and Espresso Maker

by AeroPress

☆☆☆☆☆ ▾ 5,228 customer reviews

| 292 answered questions

Price: $29.95 ✓Prime

i You can earn $1.49 in 5% Back rewards with the Amazon Prime Store Card. Learn more

In Stock.

Want it Friday, May 13? Order within 19 hrs 57 mins and choose One-Day Shipping at checkout. Details

Sold by Prima Coffee and Fulfilled by Amazon in easy-to-open packaging.

Roll over image to zoom in

Product Packaging: Standard Packaging

But finding a top-selling product isn't enough – we want to know if it can be improved. So here's where you go to the reviews. Immediately you'll see people leaving questions and comments about whether the Aeropress comes with filters, and what are they made out of. As you read the reviews, you find out what people don't like even with a product that they generally love. Amazon lets you save a ton of time by sorting the reviews including allowing you to sort by the worst reviews. A common theme comes up in the reviews of the Aeropress and it's about the filters: they're not reusable and are bleached white (meaning they contain chemicals) which are unhealthy and bad for the environment.

So that's where I got my idea for a reusable and washable filter for the Aeropress, which was the first product we launched at Crucial Coffee. I found something that was wildly popular and then identified a solution that would improve that product significantly. You can do this with absolutely any market: yoga pants, CrossFit shorts, and on and on. It's fundamental that you look at reviews of products as they hold the important insights into the faults of great products. A lot of sellers don't look at reviews of their products or those of competitors, and thus miss out on opportunities for greater customer satisfaction and market share.

When you type in "Crucial Coffee Aeropress filter" in Amazon, there are currently 87 reviews, three-quarters of which are 5-star reviews saying essentially that our filter makes the coffee taste better, and I can tell you, it's selling really well. So well that Amazon is one of the buyers. They approached me for exclusivity of this product, but I still own the supply chain, the intellectual property and trademark, all of which are key and a major benefit to having your own brand. Also, when you search for the Crucial Coffee Aeropress filter, Amazon pairs it with the Aeropress coffee maker itself so that you can buy the whole package. Aeropress doesn't care because they just want to sell their coffee makers. So everyone is happy[2].

I often go "shopping" on Amazon for new product ideas, or I visit the websites of Bed, Bath and Beyond, Walmart, and Target, all in the interest of finding new trends. Crucial Coffee is the result of this research.

---

[2] Crucial makes replacement parts to fit various home appliances so we have to always be careful about patents and how we phrase our listings for trademarks of other brand holders. Make sure you consult with a patent attorney if you are making something that fits another company's appliance so you can list your product in a way that doesn't violate any trademarks or patents.

CHAPTER 5

EBAY: ONE SIZE DOES NOT FIT ALL

An eBay customer is very different from an Amazon customer. Using Terapeak.com, you can do a search and see that, for instance, what comes up on eBay as top sellers for yoga pants is very different than what comes up on Amazon. Amazon customers shop at Amazon for convenience, selection, and price. eBay is strictly for the value shopper – those shopping around for the lowest price who could care less about convenience or selection. I always say the cheaper the content looks on eBay the better. This is why it's key to have your products on multiple channels, to hit different audiences. At the same time, do research before launching on a new channel like eBay in order to tailor your offerings, because one size does not fit all. I see many sellers plaster the internet with listings that are all the same. They put identical product listings on Amazon and eBay and elsewhere without acknowledging the different audiences. Would you sell a pricey bottled water, like Fiji or Evian, at a fast food chain like KFC? Of course not. One of the gifts of travel, even from one state to the next, is seeing how companies tailor their marketing. Whole Foods will market a product differently in Maryland than it does in Illinois.

Terapeak is one of the most helpful tools for researching eBay. The website connects with eBay's API, Application Programming Interface, to show you all of the information on sales of a given product or competitor. This is unbelievable. You can essentially spy on your competitors and do further product research. Don't worry, it's legal!

Note: The bids column is how many items sold for the date range selected. I usually choose 30-days to get a rich history of what has sold for a particular seller.

When I go into Terapeak, I can see what is trending on eBay. Let's return to hoverboard scooters for instance. Since they range anywhere from 200 to 2000 dollars, it's important I compare, contrast, and rank the different versions and sellers across the internet. You should take note of the different ways that the best selling items are titled and described. Since you'll want to set-up your listings differently on Amazon and eBay, using Terapeak like this is a great way to learn important keywords and generate new ideas for products.

One great way to understand the competitive landscape on eBay is to search a product and then sort by 'lowest price + free shipping.' Then click on competitors' listings and look at their feedback score and how much feedback they have. This way you can understand if they are competitors to be reckoned with. If they are, you can start grabbing market share by understanding what and how they sell.

It's incredible how much specific information Terapeak gives on eBay sellers – you can see how many of a given product a company has sold, that is what their **sell-through** is. Sell-through is typically defined as the quantity of products sold versus what is received from the manufacturer. With an online channel like Amazon or eBay, you can think of sell-through in terms of how many of a given product is sold at a price that makes a profit over a specific period of time versus how many of that product a company has in stock for sale. Just because you see sellers with lots of listings doesn't mean those sellers are making money. For due diligence, it's imperative to research and understand your product's sell-through, because once you move into a market and become another seller, the price will likely go down.

CAN YOU ADD VALUE?
CAN YOU DIFFERENTIATE YOUR PRODUCT?

Finally, let's say you've identified products that are selling well and making great profit for their companies. Now you need to do just like you would with researching Amazon review: find out what's missing.

THE BIGGEST MISTAKE YOU CAN MAKE
IN BUSINESS IS TO GUESS

With eBay, Amazon, and, up next, Google Adwords, you want to take guessing out of the equation to save you precious time and money.

CHAPTER 6

GOOGLE ADWORDS: GETTING SURGICAL

Google AdWords allows you to finetune your advertising and tailor your business by analyzing the keyword searches in Google. In this way, you can tailor your business to products that are actually in demand. Remember that a little over 40% of all product searches happen on Amazon, the remaining 60% largely take place on Google.

Anyone can begin using Google AdWords; as long as you have a Google account you can access its keyword analysis for free. Within Google Adwords there is a dropdown for tools. Within that is Keyword Planner Tool. From there you can search keywords using a phrase, website or category and extrapolate search volume data and trends.

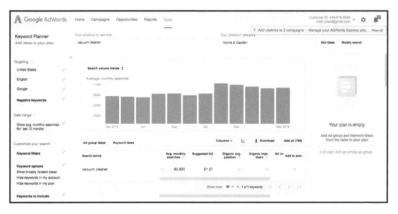

After logging in to Google AdWords (<u>adwords.google.com</u>), choose *Tools,* then *Analysis,* then *Keyword Planner.* Using the *Keyword Planner* you can see what the search volume is for certain words, and thus you can gauge the demand before going head first into making and marketing a new product. I have attached photos of a search for vacuum cleaners – clearly there is high search volume for the product. In fact Google is giving me ideas on other popular vacuum cleaner searches.

After this, you can get extremely surgical in your analysis by doing comparable searches, or *segmenting,* which is where you can, for instance, compare searches done on phones to those on desktops, or searches done on different internet browsers.

RECAP: VALIDATION IS CRITICAL

Customers are the blood of your company; without them you don't survive. Don't try to force products onto them. Instead, give them something that they are already interested in and likely to want. In terms of products and customers: it's pull, not push. We want to lure customers with a great tasting take on their favorite meal rather than force feed them a foreign food that they have yet to try. Start with your hypothesis about a potential product, and then use tools like those on Amazon, eBay, and Google AdWords to minimize your risk and validate (or invalidate) your idea.

Once my team finds out what is selling and where opportunities lie, the question becomes: Has the market already been disrupted? Can we make a profit? Is it worth our time and money to bring something to market? And the answer to all these questions leads us to sourcing.

PART 3: EXECUTION

CHAPTER 7

SOURCING: GOING DIRECT BY GOING ABROAD

When I first went to vacuum distributors to buy their accessories, I was slapped with sticker shock. I realized why so many independent brick and mortar retailers struggle to survive. An item that sold for $24 in a retail shop cost that same retailer $18 to buy from a distributor. That's virtually no wiggle room when you are take into account paying employees, rent, and taxes each year (and in e-commerce not having wiggle room costs you dearly since you have to cover shipping!) Frankly, going to a distributor felt like going to a slightly cheaper retailer – there was no flexibility on price, and thus no real opportunity to grow a business. This left me no choice but to leapfrog the distributors by getting goods straight from manufacturers. In the U.S. this is quite hard to do — America really doesn't manufacture much these days, and, as it happens, the last vacuum bag manufacturer shut its doors in 2013.

I went to the manufacturing holy land: China. First, I researched using on Alibaba.com. It's like Chinese Amazon except that it has the added benefit of also being a marketplace for business-to-business services. Take a look at this quick search I did for suppliers/makers of the iPhone 6 case which resulted in over 1,700 suppliers and 139 purchasing agents.

It was at Alibaba that I first began making a list of suppliers that could make a product I wanted, getting their prices and then getting samples of their products. Let's pause for a quick business history lesson with China that will save you a lot of money. When China's manufacturing skyrocketed 30 years ago, many factory managers didn't speak English well enough to do business with foreign partners. The role of the modern-day *Trading Company* was born. Trading companies have existed for centuries — it's essentially a middleman or an English-speaking broker who negotiates deals with Chinese manufacturers and merchants. The problem with using a Trading Company, of course, is that they take a cut of the business deal, making things instantly more expensive – and because you aren't dealing directly with the factory, you don't know the real cost of the goods being produced. Factories in China are so accustomed to doing business with foreign companies today, though, that the language barrier is far less of an issue than it used to be. Our goal is to be as close to the manufacturer as possible to get the best price, that is DIRECT.

On the internet, there are no secrets. Everything can be seen, and if it can be seen, it can be copied. In addition to Alibaba, there are various websites that are great for playing detective and finding out how your competitors made their goods and then use those same factories or similar ones to make your product: *Import Genius, Panjiva,* and *Port Examiner.* Panjiva is my favorite. In its own way, Panjiva disrupted the U.S. government's lock on import/export information by providing a solution to a broken system. Essentially, when a shipment of goods is imported into the United States, there is a *bill of lading* issued, which is an antiquated term for a receipt. There are so many bills of lading issued daily that the American government can't keep up so they give all of the receipts to Panjiva for free. Panjiva then processes and sorts all of the importation data, sells access to it online and sells it back to the U.S.

government in an organized fashion.

This is STRAIGHT UP *GENIUS*.

Once you are at the sourcing stage for your idea, I recommend you sign up for a free demo of Panjiva. Once you get an account, do some searches. If you type in 'Lululemon', you can sort all of the various products imported by Lululemon, who makes them, and the date they were imported. With a large company like Lulu, there are a variety of manufacturers in different countries. I just did a search on Panjiva for Lululemon and saw a shipment of wool scarves from Quick Feat International, which it turns out is a garment production company with factories in China, Hong Kong, India and Vietnam. This particular shipment of wool scarves came from the factory in Hong Kong.

Is there a lot of volume coming in, and thus, lots of demand? And then, who makes the product? Maybe you can use the same factory or, at the very least, learn what particular city or country has the capability to produce what you are looking for. It's worth noting that much of the importation information that you can find on Panjiva is cached on Google and so available for free. Also, many public libraries have free online access to importation/exportation information. But, in the same way that I pour over Amazon and eBay, I also pour over Panjiva because it's a vital component to the validation and execution equation, so I find having a Panjiva account is indispensable.

It's important to note that your natural detective skills come into play here. A lot of popular brands aren't registered under the same names when it comes to their legal filings and that can affect what you see when you do your importation searches. So, to find out the actual ownership of a brand, I do *Tess Trademark* searches (see *Resources* page at the end of this book) to find out who owns the registered trademark. There's a popular clothing and bag company, Brooklyn Industries, that started about twenty years ago making bags for bike messengers and has since grown into a large retail chain. When you do a trademark search for Brooklyn Industries it turns out the company is called Crypto Inc.

Word Mark	**BROOKLYN INDUSTRIES**
Goods and Services	IC 018. US 001 002 003 022 041. G & S: briefcases, backpacks, shoulder bags and messenger bags. FIRST USE: 19991007. FIRST USE IN COMMERCE: 19991007
	IC 025. US 022 039. G & S: Full line of clothing. FIRST USE: 19991015. FIRST USE IN COMMERCE: 19991015
Mark Drawing Code	(3) DESIGN PLUS WORDS, LETTERS, AND/OR NUMBERS
Design Search Code	06.07.01 - Skylines
	07.03.08 - Buildings, industrial; Factories; Industrial establishments; Smoke stacks
	19.05.03 - Gas storage tanks; Tanks, oil (large); Tanks, storage; Water towers
	26.11.01 - Rectangles as carriers or rectangles as single or multiple line borders
Serial Number	78409357
Filing Date	April 28, 2004
Current Basis	1A
Original Filing Basis	1A
Published for Opposition	November 1, 2005
Registration Number	3048859
Registration Date	January 24, 2006
Owner	(REGISTRANT) Crypto, Inc. CORPORATION NEW YORK PO Box 466 Catskill NEW YORK 12414

There is also a way, though, to block access to import information if you are brand that imports, so don't be surprised if every company you research doesn't have its importation data available. I'm happy to show you how to do this once you are at this stage.

*

CHAPTER 8

SOURCING: STARTING SMALL AND SCRAPPY

Once you've identified factories that can produce what you want, you have to find out their lead time, that is how far in advance they need to receive orders for production. Unpredictability is the nature of business, particularly when you are just starting out, so you don't want to deal with a supplier that requires long lead times. Then you need to get samples of the product. I recommend getting at least 50 of whatever you are having made to see how consistent the quality is. I've heard of entrepreneurs who have ordered shipments of products without getting samples only to receive poor quality goods that were mostly unusable, but they had already paid for them. That brings us to two more points: payment and quantity. Many factories in China will allow 30/70, meaning that once you agree that you like the samples they've sent, you put in an order and pay for 30% of that order up front and then pay for the remaining 70% after receipt of the shipment. Some factories will have you pay 40/60. Most factories will tell you that there is a certain MOQ, *Minimum Order Quantity,* like you have to order 5000 of a given item. Whatever they say is the minimum, you simply ask if you can do a smaller order. You want to start *small and scrappy.* We are trying to take the guessing out of your venture as much as possible, to minimize your risk and investment of time and money. However, there is always a certain amount of unpredictability, so you don't want to make a big investment in production at first.

This is where relationships are key and very real. It's one thing to find a factory on Alibaba or Panjiva and then set up a Skype video call and negotiate a deal. But it's a much greater level of trust to go over to China and meet a factory owner or manager in person, give your business card with two hands in the Chinese tradition, receive the factory manager's card with two hands, and then have a beer with him, go do karaoke, and even have a foot massage together while watching the Fast and Furious 19. Not only is it part of the business culture in China to have face-to-face meetings, but I can say that anywhere in the world, the more a physical and communications gap is lessened, the more favorable the business terms. To get on a plane and fly to China may not appear at first to be *small and scrappy,* but the money you spend on the flight and a week's hotel will likely save you many thousands of dollars in both your short and long term deals.

Visiting the factory is the highest return on investment move you can make when it comes to sourcing. It's after a visit that a factory manager will be more amenable to 30/70 as opposed to 40/60, or to producing half their normal MOQ for you. Think of your vendors as partners with whom you are cultivating a long-term investment together. Finally, when you visit a factory in person, you can see whether or not they have the capability to produce your product and scale upwards in the case of greater demand, and if they are really a factory or just a trading company.

Side note: If you can negotiate a deal in the local currency, i.e., RMB, or Chinese Yuan, you will likely get better terms because you'll know the real cost of your goods. Yet most manufacturers will insist on doing all deals in U.S. Dollars.

As I alluded to earlier, I went to China not merely because of lower price, but because the manufacturing for the products I needed no longer existed in America – and know that while many factories in the U.S. will make your product, they often don't package products like factories in China will, creating another step for you to solve.

If you want to make your product in the U.S., try the website, *Maker's Row,* which has a database of over 9000 factories in the United States, most of which focus on apparel and furniture. There's also www.ThomasNet.com, which is a list of all the factories in the U.S., but it's extremely hard to navigate so, there lies a tremendous opportunity for someone to build a great database to find, source and support factories in America. Somebody, *please* go make millions on that idea!

CHAPTER 9

FULFILLMENT: TAKE A LOAD OFF

If you are at the point where you are ready to look at fulfillment, then you've likely spent months researching your business idea, validating it, and possibly even traveling abroad to look at sourcing for its production. Yet all of that work really only gets you to the point where you are ready to open the virtual doors of your business. Think of all of the work you've done up until this point as the training leading up to a marathon. Now you are toeing the starting line, about to run your race.

Fulfillment is what truly makes your company *direct* and allows you to disrupt an industry. It's also possibly where I have suffered the biggest headaches. Because of the lessons I've learned, it's where I can save you the most time, money, and hair loss.

When I first started shipping vacuum filters, I thought the only way to do so was via Priority Mail from the US Post Office for a whopping $4.99. As a result, I couldn't understand how other companies were making money given that high cost. How was it that they were sending a product for free (no shipping charges) that often cost the same as the shipping itself? So the first thing I did was buy a filter from a competitor just to see how they shipped it to me. *Reverse engineering* has been a recurring theme in this book, and it's extremely beneficial when it comes to fulfillment. Simply ordering something online from another company will open your eyes to not only different types of shipment, but to different shipping presentations, the unboxing experience, and customer service. In fact, shopping online as often as possible is a good way to research. Interestingly, I recently ordered a pair of Bose ear buds, and they oddly came via UPS Ground and in a box that instantly made the package heavier and, of course, more expensive. There was lots of unnecessary packaging material for an item that weighs maybe two ounces which increased the weight and made the ear buds far more expensive to ship. This is dumb – why ship something that weighs only a couple of ounces in a 1lb UPS ground box? Fortunately for you and me, it's this type of antiquated thinking by the large incumbent companies that reveals how they still haven't grasped the nature of e-commerce and shows how much room there is for disruption.

"MY BRANDS ARE AN EXTENSION OF ME. THEY'RE CLOSE TO ME. IT'S NOT LIKE RUNNING GM, WHERE THERE'S NO EMOTIONAL ATTACHMENT."

JAY-Z,
INTERVIEW WITH BEST LIFE MAGAZINE
(APRIL 2009)

The next time you order something online, take a moment to see how it's shipped. First, look at the address the company shipped from – right away you'll know whether they are using their own fulfillment center or a 3PL, which we'll cover in more detail below. Then, how does the company interact with you? Is there a personalized note, or a packing slip with instructions for making returns? In October of 2015, there was a mass shooting in a small town in southwest Oregon that made national news for several weeks. My company got an order from a family living there and one of my employees brought it to my attention, so we sent the order with a personal note expressing our solidarity and empathy for the stress they were enduring. Not that you have to go to such lengths, but I tell these anecdotes simply to say that your brand is reflected in everything you do and it's what sets you apart from competitors.

In order to discuss a pleasing customer experience, we have to address shipping – an area where I can save you a lot of time and money by simply giving you the following abbreviation: 3PL. 3PL stands for Third Party Logistics, which essentially means to outsource your warehouse, fulfillment, and shipping. There are a couple of vital reasons to do this. The first is less obvious: managing a warehouse is an entirely different skill set than what you as an e-commerce entrepreneur likely have. You got into e-commerce because of a vision for making people's lives easier, so your focus needs to be on building the brand – marketing and sourcing it, what you're good at – and not on the operations of a warehouse and the management of its employees. Truthfully, a career warehouse employee is quite different than one who works in an office. When I first started Crucial, we had a warehouse with 17 employees who gave me daily fires to put out, some as aggravating as whether or not they were actually working. Once I outsourced our warehouse to a 3PL company, we saved $10,000 in the first month on returns alone!

If I were to start all over, the most significant change I would make would be to use a 3PL from the get-go. Not only is it far less stressful, but with a 3PL there is real scalability, whereas when you have your own warehouse it's not easy to reduce or grow your shipping because it typically means firing or hiring employees. Amazingly, with a 3PL there's actually an inverse cost structure where costs go down the more you ship. With your own warehouse they would typically go up. Such a decrease in shipping costs usually comes with the renegotiation of a contract but is common among 3PL's and one of the many perks of doing business with one and having growth in business. Take a look at this graph charting how my costs went down as my orders went up once I outsourced my fulfillment:

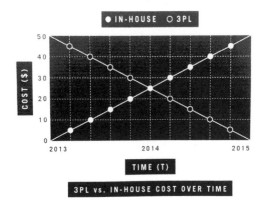

Once a 3PL is handling your business, you have no limitations on your fulfillment, but if you are doing your own shipping, growth can be a dangerous step because you won't be sure if you can meet the demand and thus risk losing customers you've worked hard to win. When it comes to choosing a 3PL, find one that can handle same day orders and high volume. And make sure they do FBA , Fulfillment By Amazon, meaning they do *Amazon FBA Workflow and Prep.* Amazon shipment creation workflow is how you get your inventory sent into Amazon's distribution center so you can offer it on Amazon Prime. Amazon has a specific workflow they need FBA shippers to follow. Many 3PLs view Amazon as a competitive threat, but as you now know, Amazon is the single largest e-commerce player, so it would be insane not to do business with them directly. If you need suggestions or introductions to 3PL companies in the U.S., or introductions to freight forwarders (shippers), feel free to contact me: chad@skubana.com.

$£¥

CHAPTER 10

FUNDING:
YOU'VE GOT
OPTIONS

Today, when people hear the terms entrepreneur, e-commerce, or start-up, it conjures images of meetings with angel investors or venture capitalists (VC), but there are many paths to funding your new company. You don't have to go to an angel or a VC, and know that if you do, they are going to take a percentage of your revenue or a percentage of your equity Also, it's not a given that you will attract or get angel/VC funding. You might have heard of people pitching their business ideas to venture capitalists with a common reaction: "We like this concept so come back in a year, and if it's doing well we can talk again about investing." VCs, like banks, are in the business of risk mitigation. They are presented with thousands of businesses for investment and from that pool they select a small handful. The good news is that if you've done your validation homework, the VC's will be blown away by your research, analysis, drive, and discipline. An angel investor is much like a film director; while they are sifting through myriad actors or candidates for their project, they are eager to choose someone. That's why an angel or VC exists – to capitalize on the growth of your idea, or simply, to invest in somebody's new company. So why not show them your validation expertise explaining why your business is likely to bring good returns over someone's social media venture that depends purely on advertising or does not yet have immediate plans for monetization. Vacuum and coffee filters, tampons, razor blade cartridges, and other e-commerce direct-to-consumer ideas aren't always sexy or flashy, but they can be extremely profitable – and, as you can see, they are necessities, not mere luxury or leisure goods. If you use a vacuum, you will need to change the filter.

Another option, instead of getting outside funding, is getting a business line of credit. Though, you want to be wary of signing a personal guarantee. Don't risk your personal assets as collateral against the loan. On that note, with whatever type of loan or funding you get, it's important to stay away from personal guarantees. It can be more difficult to get a business line of credit because it is riskier for the lender, so the interest rates are often high compared to traditional forms of business financing. There are often miscellaneous fees as well, so if you choose this route do your due diligence beforehand.

Then there's crowdfunding, an excellent way of getting capital ahead of launching your product and of further validating your product at the same time. You can think of Kickstarter (or other crowdfunding sites) as a way to fund your product before you've actually made it. You can sit back and watch people fund your first production run. I've come to believe that most people want others to succeed, particularly when someone is following their passion, and many people, even strangers, will gladly contribute a small amount of money to that end, often asking nothing in return. Examples abound. An acquaintance of mine was finishing her Master's in Filmmaking and via Facebook, she asked if all of her friends would contribute $50 so that she could raise $8000 for her thesis film. Many friends did contribute, with some giving larger amounts like $100 (still a relatively small amount of money), and this person raised over $12,000. An amount like $12,000 may be all you need to get your e-commerce business started. One of the more famous examples of crowdfunding, and one that really opened people's eyes to its power, was the 2008 Barack Obama for President campaign which relied primarily on $5 contributions, often from college students, to out-raise mega-rich donors for Hillary Clinton.

Perusing the Kickstarter or GoFundMe websites is a great way to see what people want to fund. There are always the gimmick or novelty projects like the relaunching of an oddball sci-fi show from the 90s, but often the most popular are campaigns where donors get to pre-order a unit of the very product they are helping fund. Doing a quick scroll through Kickstarter just now I see a campaign for a messenger bag that is designed for *"photographers, creatives, travelers and commuters..."* Basically, the stylish bag has compartments for cameras, camera lenses, and a laptop – it also has a strap for a tripod, a snug fit for under an airplane seat, and isn't bulky like so many other camera bags. The "Everyday Messenger™" was looking for funding of $100,000, but as of writing this, they had received close to $5 million!

It takes time and hustle to gain traction today on a popular crowdfunding site like Kickstarter, but even if your project doesn't get funded, it might be a sign that your concept needs further development or hasn't found the right audience – both of which are good wake-up calls before going all in.

"I WAS FORCED TO BE AN ARTIST AND A CEO FROM THE BEGINNING, SO I WAS FORCED TO BE LIKE A BUSINESSMAN BECAUSE WHEN I WAS TRYING TO GET A RECORD DEAL, IT WAS SO HARD TO GET A RECORD DEAL ON MY OWN THAT IT WAS EITHER GIVE UP OR CREATE MY OWN COMPANY."

JAY-Z

Finally, you can self-fund, which is how I began Crucial. Yes, there's far more risk, but also far greater reward. Ideally, you want to start small and scrappy, without great expenditure, and then build a strong foundation by putting profits directly back into the company so that you grow faster and build your brand.

CHAPTER 11

PLAYING FOR KEEPS: BE EVERYWHERE, OWN EVERYTHING

The beauty of e-commerce is that you can be everywhere. You can have multiple sales channels and do business around the world and around the clock. This sounds incredibly obvious, but you would be amazed at how many entrepreneurs only do sales on Amazon, and only in the USA. A few times in this book, I've pointed out that Amazon accounts for around 40% of product searches, which is fantastic, but that still leaves more than half the pie, 60%(!!). This is why you also want to be selling on eBay, Newegg, Sears, Rakuten (formerly Buy.com), and of course via your own website. We will get into this just ahead, but having your own shopping cart on your website is arguably the most important channel because in a sense you *own* the customer, and thus can remarket to them.

"BEING HAPPY IS THE GOAL BUT GREATNESS IS MY VISION."

CHILDISH GAMBINO,
"I'M ALRIGHT"

The reason I built Skubana was *precisely* so that I could sell on multiple channels simultaneously and effectively. I think of doing business online as akin to playing the boardgame *Monopoly*. You don't want to just have property on Park Avenue, but rather you want to own as much real estate as possible, so that means you want Park Ave, Utilities, and the Railroad. You want to be all over the board, collecting rent from everywhere, or in the case of e-commerce, be everywhere that people's eyeballs and wallets are. Amazon isn't your business. It's just a channel for your business, albeit a great one, but it's still just *a single channel.*

When I worked on Wall Street researching stocks, I would never give a vote of confidence to any company that had only one sustaining customer, and that's what entrepreneurs do to themselves when they only sell through Amazon. Committing to Amazon is understandable in that it's addictive – they make it so easy to sell your product that you don't want to bother elsewhere. But what happens if you get shut down there, as I did, losing thousands of dollars during my suspension and the appeal process. At this very moment there are Amazon sellers getting suspended without any contingency plan of how to keep making money until their suspension is resolved. Why not leverage the rest of the internet? Wouldn't the other 60% love to try your product? While you're selling on Amazon US, what about the other Amazon markets? Did you know Amazon Germany is actually the biggest Amazon channel in Europe, ahead of Great Britain, which you should also be targeting? In summary, if you're not on Amazon, you're not relevant. But if you're only on Amazon, you're losing tons of sales that someone else is winning.

Amazon is definitely the place to start your sales, almost like a product incubator. And because their standards are so high, you'll become a better seller. If you are doing well on Amazon, use those profits and insights as a bridge to reach other channels. Think of it as being a homeowner who acquires a rental property and then uses those profits to acquire another. You want to double down on your brand. As soon as you begin selling on Amazon, I would immediately create your own shopping cart on your company's website. People that find you on Amazon or elsewhere will Google you and want to know more about your company, especially if they love your product. Remember the World Aeropress Championships? We are now, for better or worse, in the era of likes. In dating profiles, you explain your style and personality by stating your favorite TV series that you binge on Netflix, and on Facebook you join the fan page of a particular brand of hot sauce, say Sriracha, for no reason other than you identify with that brand. Never before have we so willingly allied with and promoted companies and products for nothing in exchange. People want to like you and want to buy from you directly. Let them.

It's incredibly easy to set up your own shopping cart today, so there's no reason not to. I ask that while you're at it, you take a moment to look at Skubana (a detailed description is in the addendum), which enables you to run your shopping cart while also having a blast with Amazon and others. As for building your shopping cart, if you're just starting out, I recommend going with an out-of-the-box SAAS (Software as a Service) like *Bigcommerce* or *Shopify.* They have attractive themes for your shopping cart site that are ready in seconds. The best part of having another company be your SAAS shopping cart provider is that there is no up-front maintenance or developers taking longer than scheduled (and thus costing more) nor are there code-breaking issues. It's like moving into a brand new house versus building one from scratch. If you find you need more customization, go with someone like *Magento.* I'd be happy to make some introductions to contacts at the e-commerce shopping cart companies mentioned earlier – email me at chad@skubana.com and I'll do so.

Finally, it's worth noting that everything today is happening on mobile devices. That may be obvious to you, but it still amazes me that people order vacuum filters from a smartphone as opposed to from a desktop. But they do. So your website has to be responsive to smartphone and tablet orders.

CHAPTER 12
TRAFFIC

Your website and shopping cart are ready to go but how do you get people to even know about your product? Unfortunately, *build it and they will come* doesn't work on the internet, but the good news is that there are many ways to drive traffic to your site and products. First, it's vital that you capture Google searches, because as of writing this, Amazon doesn't do paid advertising. One of the best ways to capture Googlers is via the use of AdWords which were discussed earlier and are excellent low-hanging fruit, especially for your first product. I like to take advantage of Google AdWords by using Google Product Listing Ads (PLAs) which is an image of a product that Google will serve to you on Google. But Google AdWords has many, many capabilities and is very robust. You can bid on keywords, for instance, or do what's known as Sponsored Ads Management that relies on Paying Per Click. Another great use is *remarketing,* which is essentially an ad campaign that follows you as you hop around the net. Instead of text ads, remarketing utilizes image ads that are served when consumers google the appropriate keywords you're advertising against. If I google "the New York City Marathon," and then search next for "the 2016 Grammys," and navigate to a news site, I am greeted by a banner advertisement for the NYC Marathon.

Another way to generate buzz and traffic is via *affiliates* and their respective brokers. Not only do you want to spread the word about your product, but you want people to find out about your product from a source they trust. A review from a friend or an authority is prized in business and public relations because it's far more valuable than a review by a stranger or an automated advertisement. Internet or social media stars are so powerful now because of the loyalty of their audience. If Tim Ferriss promotes a book, there's a decent chance it will rocket upward in sales. It's why companies or entrepreneurs (dentists, landscapers, etc.) will often give existing clients a monetary reward if they refer a friend. Word of mouth is an unsolicited stamp of approval that spreads trust and results in new customers. One of the best ways to find influencers is via *BuzzSumo.*

But not all of us make trendy products that generate cool cocktail party convo. While profitable, vacuum filters are high on the snooze list, so I have had to get creative in targeting my audience. Entrepreneur Gary Vaynerchuk has spoken about the need to think of something from a point of view that is one step removed, meaning: *Who would benefit from your product though they might not realize it?* When I was thinking about marketing my vacuum filters, it wasn't until I stepped back that I made serious progress. *Who needs a new vacuum filter? Someone in need of really clean floors and air...* it hit me: pregnant women who were nesting and preparing their homes for a newborn would want the cleanest air possible and floors that were free of dust bunnies, so changing their vacuum filter was a priority for preparing their home for a new baby. It was then up to me to find affiliate marketers that targeted new moms– mommy bloggers and parenting websites. I also targeted allergy sufferers. With coffee filters, it was a more of a direct shot, I didn't need to go a step removed, so instead of blindly advertising on Facebook, I homed in on coffee enthusiasts via affiliates targeting sites for coffee aficionados.

Affiliate marketing sites like Pepper Jam, Share-a-sale are brokers and connect the publisher (the person that has the audience) to the people that have the product. For example – Crucial Vacuum – we have affiliate relationships with mommy bloggers and allergy sufferer sites. When they post about us, they get a cut of the sale – a % of revenue, which is typically an embedded link that gives a percentage of a sale to an individual working as affiliate – it gives them credit for the sale. Everyone drives traffic to their website and products differently. For me, it's primarily Google, but begin to think about how you float around the internet. How are you learning about books, restaurants, podcasts and other products? Sometimes when you sign up to subscribe to a website's newsletter or to fill out an online RSVP to attend an event, you might be presented with a question like *How did you hear about us?* – after jogging your memory for how you ended up at that site, you select from a list of sources like Facebook, Google, etc.

"THE FACT IS THAT YOU CAN'T HIT
A TARGET THAT YOU CAN'T SEE. IF
YOU DON'T KNOW WHERE YOU
ARE GOING, YOU WILL PROBABLY
END UP SOMEWHERE ELSE."

ZIG ZIGLAR

CHAPTER 13
SOCIAL
MEDIA

Everything we do today on social media is branding and marketing. Our posts are extremely curated to present the version of ourselves we want the world to have – be it ironic, hardworking, boastful, sexy, proud, self-deprecating, celebratory, comedic, vulnerable, or even hurt. When we put a photo or status out into the world the intent is clear: relate to me. You know what will generate loops, regrams, reposts, likes, retweets, and new followers for you, or perhaps what will bring you unwanted attention. At the same time, you also know what feels forced, when your personal brand, or that of a friend's or a stranger's or celebrity's, is straying too far from the truth. That most of us have spent the last five plus years engaging with the world virtually means we have all developed a tremendous sensitivity (intolerance) for bullshit in social media marketing. Bullshit in social media marketing is just like bullshit in advertising on TV or radio or anywhere else. People find a way to tune it out as soon as they recognize it. From the moment you broadcast yourself or your company, your message must be one of real value if you intend for your followers to actually stop and listen.

"REAL RECOGNIZE REAL"

JAY-Z,

"ALL AROUND THE WORLD"

I'm not a social media expert. There many others, Tim Ferriss in particular (http://fourhourworkweek.com/2014/07/21/harrys-prelaunchr-email/), who have great blogs about concrete strategies for upping social media presence on the various networks. In this section, I'm merely going to offer a few thoughts on social media, the main one being that when thinking about your current or future company's social media presence, constantly observe how you like to be marketed. Few of us enjoy spam emails, squeeze pages, pop-ups, and emails from auto-responders, or appreciate our emails being sold to third parties, or the false depiction of a scarcity of products.

To develop a truly loyal fanbase, I recommend that content marketing be your focus. Content marketing is defined as creating and distributing relevant and valuable content to attract, acquire, and engage a clearly defined and understood target audience – with the objective of driving profitable customer action. One of the best ways to do that is via vlogs or videos on YouTube, which is owned by Google and, thus, indexes really well on Google. As of this writing, YouTube is currently getting over 4 billion pageviews a day and that number keeps growing – and don't forget that it's the 2nd most popular search engine after Google. On Amazon, there's really no place to do demonstrations or have greater interaction with your audience, but with content marketing your audience gets to know you and your story and why you created your product you did. Your website and content sites like YouTube are your platform to present yourself or your business as the expert on a subject and to dial in on your value propositions and offer value in ways that Amazon cannot.

With all that said, here are some specific social media content marketing guidelines:

1. *Give Before You Receive.* Always add value and pump the market with content, taking a long view approach of at least the next two years to develop a core sea of followers and fans.

2. *Be Helpful.* Solve a problem, take a worry and turn it into a smile. You'll get your email opened, make a friend, and nurture a customer relationship that will pay dividends for a long time to come. Only once you have a captive audience that respects you and knows you have integrity can you start pushing promo codes.

3. *The Rule of 10.* For every 10 items of content (blogs/videos/posts) delivered, nine should be giving something for free to an audience, and one should ask the audience to do (pay for) something. At the end of every content item (YouTube post, blog, etc.), though, you may do a quick upsell of whatever you are currently promoting.

4. *Consistency.* Marketing content should be consistent, but doesn't have to follow a rigid schedule, especially when you are starting out. In fact, it is best for content not to have military rigidity so that the audience feels that the content is real. Note: most people start these endeavors, particularly blogging and blogging, only to give up after a month or two. If that's you, or you don't have the budget to get someone else to do your content for you, don't bother getting started. It may take a full year of weekly three-minute YouTube videos before your audience goes from the hundreds to the tens of thousands. But that's what makes YouTube still a great platform — most people give up and don't build an audience, so if you stick with it, the dividends will be significant. Know that content is king. It's far better to have a steady stream of even low-tech content with a quality message than one or two expensive videos or lengthy blogs but then a drop in presence.

5. *Maintain Multiple Platforms, but Respect Each as Unique.* Just as eBay is different from Amazon, Snapchat's users are different from Instagram's, but both might be viable platforms to promote your product either through content or advertising. So it follows that since every social media platform is unique, not all social media will be appropriate for your e-commerce company. The key is to simply hang out at the different sites or apps and see what trends and content are relevant to your product even if it's one step removed. When I started wading in the social media pool, I found that no one cared about dirty vacuum filters on Pinterest, but interestingly, Twitter is rife with people complaining about mediocre and damaged filters, so on Twitter I had a built-in audience for Crucial Vacuum.

6. *It's About Friends.* In the same way that a customer is so much easier to market to than non-customers, your friends and family are your most devoted fans and promoters when starting out. You must ask in sincere emails for their help and recognition of your month's of hard work by liking your Facebook page, retweeting your content promo codes and so on. Your network wants to help you and see you become a great success, so when they tell their friends, you will develop a respectable audience. This is also your opportunity for validation. If you tell ten friends about your idea, and none of them shows the slightest enthusiasm, your idea needs more work. What's true for you in terms of wants and needs is likely true for them and vice versa.

7. *Be a Niche Player.* The more niche of a category your product falls into, the better chance it has on social media. From the earliest iterations of the internet, there were people creating fan clubs (remember Yahoo! Groups?) for their favorite hobbies and products. We often celebrate online that which is niche because there aren't enough people around us in the flesh that share our particular passion. In earlier chapters, I've detailed how ardent coffee fans are in their love for the AeroPress Coffee Maker, to the point that they hold championships around the world for best AeroPress brewed coffee – that is all thanks to niche fans finding each other on social media. Seth Godin often talks about how, when we travel, we can find our tribe, be it at a CrossFit gym or a vegan restaurant, whether in Amsterdam or in Sydney, thanks to social media. Niche fans are far more loyal, so while we may fantasize about having Kim Kardashian's 60 million Instagram followers, it might actually prove more lucrative to have 50,000 followers eagerly anticipating your new releases.

8. *Keep it Light.* People go on social media as an escape, so it's really more of a place to entertain than make sales. It's really your opportunity to further develop your brand and identity. If you can entertain and engage first, then the sales will pour in! Gary Vaynerchuk took over his parents' liquor store in 1998 and massively grew the business thanks in large part to hilarious yet low budget daily videos that were part of a series called Wine Library TV where Gary did wine tastings and provided colorful commentary on the wines. You can buy wine from many places, but people sought out Gary's store because of his charm and expertise. His rise in popularity was so great that he was soon asked to be on the David Letterman show, and that was years before Gary started vlogging and speaking about entrepreneurship.

9. *Stay Narrow.* When possible, seek out curated sites and influencers. If you make a surfboard accessory, target surfing websites or surfing experts on YouTube with a large following and do the same on the rest of social media. Find your tribe.

CONCLUSION
LOOKING
FORWARD

It's Friday around 5 p.m. here at Skubana HQ. The vibe is celebratory: a refrigerator door swings open and shut, then back open. Beer bottles clink. The laughter meter rises. Yet, if I look around, no one is punching out. More than a kick-off to the weekend, the buzz feels like a celebration of the week that was. High-fives for problems and puzzles solved – and for new Skubana users turned believers. I came to e-commerce seven years ago in part because the opportunity presented itself and more importantly because I knew I didn't want to go back to Wall Street to be someone's underling. What happened soon after with Crucial Vacuum far surpassed my original goals. I quickly achieved financial success that continues to improve year upon year. In reality, the bulk of my team no longer works on Crucial, as that brand practically runs itself. They're instead focused on building and perfecting our business web software, Skubana.

I say this to emphasize that I could've rested awhile ago. Monetarily, I'm not hurting, but my entrepreneurial spirit, my hunger to disrupt and to make better, simpler products and more accessible solutions keeps me excited for tomorrow. It's that desire to learn, grow, and hustle that I look for far above prestige degrees when I interview potential employees. I look for doers who can get the job done. There are lots of smiles here in my office now, but they're the kind you see on faces after a marathon or a boot camp workout. We haven't made it to the summit yet, but we're tickled by thoughts of what the view will be like. You have to enjoy the climb, because once you reach the tip of one peak, are you going to call it quits? You must find another mountain. Delight in the work and get lost in it. I guarantee you that once you start earning a nice paycheck from your toil, the money won't sustain you to keep going, but joy for the work, for solving problems, for helping people will. It's cliché now, I know. You must be tired of hearing people who have tasted success and riches tell you that money isn't enough. Once again: it's true. Entrepreneurship is a sport – there are lots of highs and lows and money isn't a big enough high. Rather, there's your creative legacy – what mark are you leaving on the world? What's the example you are leaving for your community? To strike out on your own takes tremendous strength and courage, so why not make your impact a lasting one? Take pride in your efforts and have fun along the way.

Having advised and taught various entrepreneurs over the years, I know that you will find considerable success if you follow the methods in this book. Your hustle will be such that once your first goal posts are reached, you will set new ones. If you simply hope to have an automated business that runs itself, I still applaud you for achieving your dream and for your hard work getting there.

My wish, then, is that along your journey you will cultivate a love for a concept that is now dear to me: *reciprocity*. As an entrepreneur, there's absolutely no way you can survive entirely on your own – at every turn you will have to form relationships and thus be presented with opportunities to help others. As with your customers, if you can help your partners and fellow entrepreneurs, there's no question people will be eager to help you do the same. Over the last several years I've been aided in myriad ways, so now when meeting people, I try to think about how I can help them. Hopefully this book is of considerable help to you. It would give me great joy to know that it was. Similarly, if you think it could be improved, or find yourself struggling in your e-commerce endeavor, please contact me and I shall do my best to be of service to you.

I often sign my emails *Looking Forward* not only because of the lightning speed of business and the need to stay a step ahead, but more because of the role that chance and opportunity play in life, even when there are bumps and deviations in the road. I believe that you have found this book at your own opportune moment and I wish you a path filled with enough challenge to make you relish both the unforeseen obstacles and the opportunities that are born from navigating them.

Looking forward,
Chad Rubin

ADDENDUM:
SKUBANA

Software and technology are the absolute backbone of any e-commerce business. To build an e-commerce business without a robust software platform is like putting up a house without a foundation. I've already described why I was in need of a solution like Skubana. It was born from fear, pain, and frustration. As an Amazon seller, I would be riding the highest highs one moment and not able to sleep at night the next. I was kicked off Amazon twice because my various software tools didn't interact with one another. The reality is that if you are running 6 separate softwares, it's going to get ugly. It did, and I knew I had a problem that many other e-commerce entrepreneurs had too. I needed a software that was cloud-based that could run my company on its own – an all-in-one solution. Frankly, I wouldn't have built it if something else had existed that could run my business.

So in the simplest terms, let's look at the main problem: When you are using multiple solutions to run your business, you don't have any ongoing true view of your data. This is so much more vital than merely having an actualized tally of inventory. It's imperative that you have a true view of your business data in order to make smart business decisions. When you have a single cloud-based software that's running your business and unifying your data from all of your various sales channels, you have access to every touch point in your business at a moment's notice.

INITIAL COSTS	COMPREHENSIVE COSTS
HOW DO MANY AMAZON SELLERS UNFORTUNATELY THINK ABOUT 'COST'?	...MEANWHILE,
+ WHOLESALE COST + INBOUND / OUTBOUND SHIPPING + AMAZON COMMISSIONS + FBA FEES	• OVERHEAD COSTS • HIDDEN COSTS ARE CONSOLIDATED AT END OF YEAR, AND SUBTRACTED FROM TOTAL PROFIT
= $ PROFIT...	

If you use a solution today that has a desktop shipper or another shipping solution that's not part of the actual end-to-end software, how do you know what your true profit per SKU (stock item) is? Sellers are often focused on the top-line (sales) and see money coming in, but the question is: *are you making money?* It's even more difficult if you are an FBA seller; Amazon doesn't always make it easy. You need to find your *true profit* above all costs (commission costs, dormant fees, storage fees, weight-based fees, shipping costs, indirect *and* overhead costs). What's your true profit per SKU? Skubana is here to help.

EXAMPLE:

- OVERHEAD COSTS SPECIFIC JUST TO AMAZON = $20K

- OTHER OVERHEAD COSTS APPLIED TO YOUR OVERALL BUSINESS = $175K

- TOTAL UNITS SOLD = 100K

- PORTION OF TOTAL UNITS SOLD ON AMAZON = 80%

- TOTAL AMAZON OVERHEAD = (80% • $175K) + 20K = $160K

- OVERHEAD PER AMAZON UNIT SOLD = $160K . 80K UNITS = $2.00

Let's say you're selling on Amazon FBA. You log on to Seller Central and Amazon gives you your sales settlement every 2 weeks. The money rolls into your bank account. But they don't answer the other question which asks: are you actually making money? I talk to hundreds of sellers a week, and I ask them, "Are you making money on Amazon?" and "How do you know if you are profitable on Amazon FBA?" The sad reality is that most sellers know more about their cars than they do about their business. How many miles on your car? How many miles to the gallon?

When is the next tune-up? What did you buy the car for? Yet most entrepreneurs can't tell me what their specific profits are and certainly not per item.

It's not their fault. If Amazon reported the true profits to sellers, there would be a revolt. Sellers would wake up and realize they can't drop their prices to where they are since it's not sustainable. Many sellers would realize they are really making money for Amazon, but not for themselves. I used to hire a former Amazon executive turned consultant to put together a SKU profitability report every 6 months. He would report to me all of my returns for all of my FBA SKUs and what my dormant fees were for every SKU. This took him several hours every week to manually calculate these metrics in spreadsheets, and he charged me several thousand bucks every 6 months. It wasn't a small amount of money, but is several grand worth it in order to make or save $100K? Of course, it is. These metrics are critical to my business. When it was time to put together Skubana, I hired James to be a part of my team so that every Skubana user would have this kind of capability. We had developers spend months poring over Amazon reports in order to find all kinds of hidden fees that cripple businesses and severely limit their profits: dormant fees, return fees, and many more. We implemented these analytical tools into Skubana and the instant Skubana was created, legions of e-commerce entrepreneurs have jumped at the opportunity to use it and then spread the word to their entrepreneur buddies in order to save countless hours of precious time and gobs of money. What made Skubana so conducive to sharing (and what grew our customer base completely by word-of-mouth) was the immediacy of the solution.

```
THE HIDDEN COSTS ON AMAZON

x AMAZON'S REFUND COMMISSION FEE

x FBA REFUND SHIPPING: FROM
CUSTOMER TO FULFILLMENT CENTER
(FOR CERTAIN CATAGORIES)

x FBA DISPOSAL FEES, OR FEES FOR
RETURN SHIPPING FROM FULFILLMENT
CENTER TO SELLER

x THE SELLER'S INTERNAL PROCESSING/
HANDLING FEES

x THE SELLER'S WRITE-DOWN / WRITE-
OFF COSTS

x ANY OPPORTUNITY COSTS OF
STOCK-OUTS
```

BE EVERYWHERE AND KNOW HOW YOU'RE PERFORMING

I sell on 15 channels. When more channels appear, I will likely sell on those too. If Amazon were the only channel in town, that would be sufficient, but there's a huge chunk of e-commerce real estate that Amazon doesn't cover. I want your company to be able to sell on as many channels as you would like and to know how each of your products are doing on every channel. Skubana breaks down every channel you are selling on to see where there are holes in your bucket.

TECHNOLOGY STACK CHECKLIST

Whether you choose to go with Skubana or another software to run your business, there are some absolute musts:

1. **Your software shouldn't take a cut of your revenue.**

Think about it: It doesn't matter to a server, whether your order value is $1 or $100. It's still the same processing power to process that transaction. Don't give away your revenue.

2. **There should be no contract.**

Don't lock yourself into a contract that you can't get out of. The contract is there to protect the vendor, not you.

3. **You must be on the cloud and operate in real time.**

You can't use legacy tools to build a business for the future. Make sure it's on the cloud and unified so it's real-time.

4. **Ask: Is it customizable for your business?**

Make sure it is multi-marketplace, multi-channel enabled. Not a one-trick pony.

5. **Your software must have the capacity to allow you to grow your company.**

It has gotta be scalable.

6. **Always try before you buy.**

You have to test drive the car before you buy it.

7. **There should be no set-up fees and no custom development.**

No code to have your developers fiddle with.

Just as you want to provide products and services for your customers that are better, cheaper, easier and direct, so should you expect the same from your providers and your technology platforms. That should hold true in every facet of your business. Transparency and ease is the way to do business today. Your growth ceiling should not be limited by the software you invest in. If you are a seller today, ask yourself: Where am I spending my time, and how can I automate my business so that I can scale and grow? If you are an FBA seller, there's a much better use of your time than going through thousands of line items each day to create Amazon Seller reports on Excel.

When you think about creating your business, you also need to think about exiting your business, that is selling it. That means creating a highly profitable company that's doing business across many channels that is constantly growing. The right software can greatly aid your ability to do that so that you can one day sell your company at a value that is far greater than your yearly revenue.

Skubana was designed for those that want to grow, that want to disrupt. If you are merely looking to solely sell on one channel with only a couple of products and sell casually, then Skubana is not for you. On the other hand, if your company is in need of real business intelligence tools for doing big business across multiple channels, then Skubana is for you.

Skubana is hands down the business venture that I am most proud to be a part of. I could write many more pages about Skubana's myriad benefits, but the best way to understand its power is for you to visit www.skubana.com and try Skubana for free. We put three years into making what I believe is the finest end-to-end software for managing any e-commerce business and we are constantly working to make it even better. Everyone at Skubana is eager to help you get the maximum benefit from our software so that your company can flourish, and I pride myself on instilling in my help team, which includes myself, with the utmost respect for our customers.

Feel free to contact me directly if you want to discuss the benefits of Skubana further.

Looking forward,
Chad Rubin

I applaud you for making it through to the end and hopefully you have launched or are about to launch a disruptive e-commerce business.

Please remember to pick up my free toolkit, Amazon Mastery: 10 Crucial Strategies from a Top 200 Seller. (ecommercerenegade.com/bonus) to help you avoid mistakes when using the world's top online store. It is my thanks to you for buying this book.

Chad Rubin

IT TAKES A VILLAGE

Nothing I do is possible without the support of my family. My incredible life companion and wife, Shira Turkl-Rubin, my soulmate who empowers me to accomplish everything I want and taught me how to love...and my cat Kali who unconditionally supports us.

I'm grateful for my parents Nancy and Gerald Rubin who instilled me with a sense that anything is possible and prohibited the word can't from entering my vocabulary. The disruptive nature of this book is an absolute product of my upbringing.

Thanks to my sister Shana Freeman for always being selfless and her husband Sam Freeman for always being insightful and strong.

I wish to give tremendous thanks to Peter Turkl, my other father and teacher, for his consistent support and help shaping and modeling these businesses. You helped me hone and focus my business acumen into cohesion.

Ruth Samuel, thanks for your unwavering support and love throughout this journey.

Thank you to my entire ancestry who risked everything to provide me with an opportunity to build a better future.

Massive thank you to the Crucial and Skubana team for always keeping me on point and helping me pursue (and achieve) my dreams. Special thanks to Kristin Leishman and Cindy Yuk for helping us attain extraordinary growth and for being my backup brain. Ann Burgos, could not manage everything without you.

Thank you DJ Kunovac, co-founder of Skubana, for pushing the limits of what is possible.

My gratitude goes out to the Skubana Investors who believed in us when we had zero customers and this was all just an idea. Jay Goldberg, thank you for being a true inspiration and mentor for me.

I would also like to extend my thanks to everyone that helped critique, proofread, and review this book: Jay Goldberg, Willie Tsang, Jane Freeman, James Thomson, Andrew Muller, Ben Stein, Ryan and Mika Oakes, Noah Zide, and Tristan Clausell

Lastly, thanks to the co-writer of this book, Frank Turner, involved in this book from the beginning. For all his help, I thank him warmly.

Nils Davey, thank you for your wonderful book cover and inner illustrations and Josh Raab for guiding me through the final detail-obsessive editing process along with the entire publishing process.

YEAH, THIS ALBUM IS DEDICATED TO ALL THE TEACHERS THAT TOLD ME I'D NEVER AMOUNT TO NOTHING, TO ALL THE PEOPLE THAT LIVED ABOVE THE BUILDINGS THAT I WAS HUSTLING IN FRONT OF THAT CALLED THE POLICE ON ME WHEN I WAS JUST TRYING TO MAKE SOME MONEY TO FEED MY DAUGHTER, AND ALL THE NI**AS IN THE STRUGGLE. YOU KNOW WHAT I'M SAYING. IT'S ALL GOOD BABY BABY.

NOTORIOUS BIG

RESOURCES

Sourcing

Alibaba.com

Import Genius.com

Panjiva.com

Port Examiner.com

Tess Trademark
(http://tmsearch.uspto.gov/bin/gate.exe?f=tess&state=4802:ypi713,1,1)

Maker'sRow.com

ThomasNet.com

Funding

Kickstarter.com

GoFundMe.com

Traffic

BuzzSumo.com

Pepperjamnetwork.com

Shareasale.com

Questions?

Visit Skubana.com or email chad@skubana.com